New Vision Ministries Presents:

God Loves You

Written By Eric Johnson

Most of the scripture verses from God's word within this book have been blended with the Holy Spirit's anointing and modern clarity to enable the reader to understand and apply the truth to their lives.

ISBN-13: 978-0692445440 (Eric Johnson)

Table Of Contence

Introduction

God loves us unconditionally, therefore there is nothing that you can do that would make him love you more and there's nothing that you can do that would make him love you less. God is love. It's his nature to love without restraint or conditions. His love is unchanging. He won't love us any better when we become better. He loves us one hundred percent right now as we are. God's love for us is higher than the Heavens are above the earth. Psalm 103:11

His love does not change even if we have no plans to change. What needs to change is our ability to receive his love. So the choice is yours, will you open your heart to him right now and receive more of his love than you've ever experienced before? Give him your whole heart today child of God. Give him your depression, pain and unforgiveness that has held you back and kept you down. God will minister peace and give you rest on all sides. God loves us one hundred percent as we are right at this moment. So allow yourself to be loved by him completely.

He adores us. He's crazy about us. He wants us to live like people who are outrageously loved. God wants us to understand, receive and express this radical, out of this world type of love. His love comes to set us free from rejection, shame, low self-esteem, despair and self-abuse.

When God looks at us, he sees someone who he loves very much. Yes a good father would certainly be disappointed in some of their children's choices because he knows it could hurt them, but his love for that child is never in question.

God has so much to say to us and so many places to take us in his heart. But we can't go there unless we allow him to love us completely. His love for us will break every barrier and crush every wall that we've built around ourselves. God's love is the most power force that has ever touched the human heart. So allow yourself to be loved.

GOD LOVES YOU
I finally discovered how valued I was...
when I personally met God's love.

Most parents have those baby books where they record when their baby first smiled at them or when they first rolled over from their back to their belly. Many times people just write down how much they love that new child of theirs. I was reading in my daughter Courtney's baby book a while back. She was only about seven months old when I wrote this:

Courtney you're so pretty. You have these big beautiful blue eyes and I just love looking into them. You smile all the time and make everyone around you smile also. You are a very quiet baby, you almost never cry. You have a beautiful voice and love to clap your hands. You are always content just looking around and exploring, you discover new things everyday. I love to watch you when you're sleeping. I love to see you enjoy all the many new experiences in life. I think you've finally discovered that your voice is beautiful. It's like you enjoy listening to yourself talk and laugh. You completely mesmerize me. Your face captures my complete attention. I can't keep myself from coming in the room and wrapping my arms around you and saying you're mine and I love you. You fill my life with such joy.

Your Dad

I was just bawling my eyes out when I read this. It brought back so many wonderful memories for me. It helped me to remember just how much I was completely in love with her. I loved both my daughters the moment I laid eyes on them. My love for them didn't have to grow or mature, it was instantaneous. I'm so glad I took the time to write about them. Now all these many years later they can read in their baby books and understand just how much their mom and I treasured our time with them.

It's the same way with God's word (the Bible); he has written a lot about how much he loves us. Here is what he's written about us.

MY LITTLE CHILD

You are my creation and you stand blameless before me. Rom. 5:1,6:1-6

I have chosen you and adopted you, because I love you. I'm so glad you're a part of my family. You are very precious to me. Allow me to influence you just as a potter shapes their clay. Jeremiah 18:6

I want you to know me as completely as I know you. Ephesians 1:8 & 17

Because you are mine, my spirit lives in you. You shall have my mighty power and favor with you all the days of your life. Ephesians 1:18, 2:5 & 6

I am anxious to hear your voice everyday. Ephesians 2:18, 3:12

I have forgiven you yesterday, today and tomorrow completely. The debt and curse against any child of mine has been lifted. Colossians 1:13 14

2

My grace and mercy will always be with you. Heb. 4:16

My spirit in you will be like a counselor that leads you throughout your day. I will teach you to have patience, kindness, gentleness and self control. Galatians 5:22

I see so much potential in you. Philippians 2:13

You are the apple of my eye. Zechariah 2:8

I have placed my seal on you and I will not remove it. Nothing will snatch you out of my hand. Ephesians 1:4 & 13, 2:19

Your face reflects the light of my love. Colossians 1:13

Your countenance will break forth like the dawn; it will shine like the midday sun. Psalm 37:6

I have created you, formed you and redeemed you. You are mine forever. Isaiah 43:1

I trust you with the secret knowledge of my kingdom. I Chronicles 4:1

I've placed my royal family seal on you, so that everyone will know that you are a child of the king. II Corinthians 1:22

I have anointed and equipped you for every good purpose that I have ordained for you. II Timothy 1:7, 3:17

When I look at you, I see a person completely free from sin. Just as if you've never sinned. I have covered you with my righteousness. Romans 5:1

Your new life contains the power of my spirit. I will put my words in your mouth and I will cover you with the shadow of my hand. Isaiah 51:16

Your thoughts will be like my own thoughts.
Romans 8:4, 12:2

You are going to prosper and have a divine future.
Jeremiah 29:11

Don't ever forget my child, that I choose you, you are
royalty, you are apart of my heavenly family.
You belong to no one else but me. I Peter 2:9

Nothing will ever separate you from my love. Rom. 8:39

Since your spirit has been purged from sin, your body,
mind and soul are now instruments of righteousness.
Romans 6:13

My shield of favor will protect you all the days of your life.
I Peter 1:3 & 4

I will lavish you with wisdom and understanding beyond
your years. You will know the mystery of my will
and what pleases me. Ephesians 1:8 & 9

You are my wonderful handiwork.
I am so proud to call you my own. Ephesians 2:10

When you call out to me, I will always answer you.
Psalm 91:15

You wear a ring of comfort and joy on your finger.
Jeremiah 31:13

You will rule over the many works of my hands
and I will lay everything at your feet. Psalm 8:6

I want you to resemble me by reflecting my love,
forgiveness and grace to others. II Corinthians 3:18

I will shield you with my hand of protection
as I lay it on your head. Psalm 3:3

I have crowned you with love and compassion;
I will satisfy your desires with my favor
and blessings. Psalm 103:4 & 5

I will protect you all the days of your life
so that no harm will come to you. Psalm 91:10 & 14

I will never leave you or forsake you. Hebrews 13:5

From your Father who loves you more than anything.
John 3:16

There are so many wonderful things that God has said about us in the bible. I hope you're beginning to grasp how much God loves you. God promises in his word that if we will start taking the steps to understand his character, he will reveal himself to us in a way we can understand.

I read my daughters' baby books to them every once in a while so they will understand how much I love them. They love hearing about themselves and all the little things we noticed about them when they were babies. From the very first day I saw them, I loved them, because they are mine. They are mine to love, hold, nurture, teach and enjoy. They are a part of me. I get to help mold them and shape them into who they will become.

God loves us the way he does because we're his. You are his to hold, love, nurture, teach and enjoy. All the information you just read about yourself is from God's word (The Bible). God wouldn't have put it there if he didn't mean it. When we spend time seeking his face, reading about his character in the bible or worshiping him, then that's when he reveals his love to us in a greater way. Make sure you go back and read the words of *MY LITTLE CHILD* as often as you can, so that your constantly reminded of how much God loves you.

SPIRITUAL VISION – The Voice Of Love

This really happened to me. One morning many years ago when I was waking up out of my sleep, I had this incredible experience with God. I was standing in this thick cloud of fog wondering where I was. Then someone spoke to me out of the cloud, he asked me a question. His voice was loud and commanding. He said, "Who are you?" I knew then it was God speaking to me. I never had anything happen to me like this before. How was I going to answer God? I'd better tell him the truth for sure; I mean it was God speaking directly to me. What was the answer to the question he was looking for? I just spoke what was in my heart. I said, "NOT MUCH." Then the Lord said something to me that I'll obviously never forget for the rest of my life. He said,

"Did I send my Son...for NOT MUCH?"

At that moment it was like information was flowing into my head at a thousand miles an hour. God wrote a love letter to me as thick as a phone book. It was like he placed it on the top of my head and said, "Receive this now from me in your understanding." It was one of the most incredible moments of my life. Some type of channel had been opened and heavenly wisdom began transforming my mind. The information was about me. It was important knowledge about who I was in Christ. It was the most intense manifestation of God I had ever felt. At that moment I finally realized how much God loves and cares for me. God revealed to me the truth about his nature. I was just as awake, after he said that to me, as I am right now writing this book. The intensity of the meeting was so powerful...I'll remember it forever.

GOD JUST SPOKE TO ME!

It was the closest I had ever come to actually hearing the audible voice of God. I mean I really did hear the voice of God; it's just that I happened to be sleeping just before this event. He touched me with an undeniable love from Heaven that I'll never be able to describe in words.

The bible does describe this kind of love. I've compiled four bookmarkers that will help you understand how much God loves you. They are <u>GOD KNOWS MY NAME</u>, <u>I AM</u>, <u>BY GOD'S GRACE</u> and <u>MY LITTLE CHILD</u>. After that event, I never again doubted what God says about me in his word. I hope you understand that God loves you with the exact same relentless passion.

Faith works by love. Galatians 5:6
(You can only operate in faith, if you're operating in love.)

Won't you try this today? Get down on your knees right now and allow the love of God to absorb into every area of your spirit. Let God fill every cell in your brain with the fact that he's completely in love with you. Tell God you want to completely understand how much he loves you and to fill you with his unconditional, unlimited and unwavering love. When he does this, AND HE WILL, the love of the Lord will take over every part of your character. **Your circumstances might be the same tomorrow but your heart will be different. All your hurts, heavy burdens, emotional strife and confusion will slowly dissolve as the love of God flows into your heart.** It's kind of like putting a garden hose, flowing with water, into a jar filled with dirt. The rush of clear clean water will eventually remove all the dirt from the vessel. There will soon be an overflow out of your vessel and it will have an undeniable effect on the people around you. It will be like a tremendous waterfall pouring into you and then flowing out of you (John 7:38). God's greatest desire is for you to UNDERSTAND his love, RECEIVE his love and then GIVE his love to others. **The love of God is the single most important discovery you'll ever make in life.** The world would be lost without the love of God. Let's read a little bit about God's love from I Corinthians 13.

THE DETAILS OF GOD'S LOVE

Love endures long and is patient and kind.
Love is never envious,
it never boils over with jealousy.
It isn't boastful. It does not display
itself in a prideful haughty way.
It's not conceited, arrogant or
inflated with pride. It's not rude.
God's love in us does not insist on its own way.
It's not self-seeking, touchy, grouchy or resentful.
It takes no account of the evil done to it.
Love pays no attention to a suffered wrong.
It grieves at injustice and unrighteousness
and rejoices when righteousness and truth prevail.
Love bears up under anything and
everything that comes our way.
It's always ready to believe for the best
in every person. It's hopes are fadeless under all
circumstances and endures everything without
weakening. Love never fails. It never fades
away or gives up. I Corinthians 13:4-8

God has poured out his love into our hearts
by the Holy Spirit. Romans 5:5

May God strengthen you with his power in your spirit,
because God has rooted and established you in love.
You can know without a doubt, how wide, how long, how
high and how deep are the dimensions of God's love for
you. His love surpasses anything you've ever came in
contact with before. Know this child of God; God has
completely filled you with his love in your inner being.
You have the fullness of God's divine nature
residing in you. Ephesians 3:16-19

9

God's love is already in every born-again Christian. We just need to trust him with it, then it can burst forth out of you like a volcano. It may already be coming out of you in new ways and desires that were never there before. Reading God's word will help unleash God's love from within you. You have to know that all of God's love is in you before it can come out of you. The words "*God loves you*" echoed from every one of Jesus' actions. That's why he taught us, healed us and eventually died for us.

Even though the mountains could be shaken flat and the hills crumble to the ground, never will my unfailing love for you be shaken says the LORD. Isaiah 54:10

I used to demonstrate to my daughter Erika how much I loved her by saying, "I love you this much." Then I would hold out my hands in front of her and slowly spread them out as wide as I could. I used to do this all the time so she could see visually how much I loved her. God describes his love for us in a similar way. The following verse is God speaking:

As high as the Heavens are above the earth…
so great is my love for you. Psalm 103:11

God's love is so vast, it really is OUT OF THIS WORLD! In this scripture God describes for us the physical dimensions of his love, just like I did with my daughter Erika. The speed of light travels at around three hundred million meters per second (300,000,000 meters/second). That equates to five trillion, nine hundred billion miles per year (5,900,000,000,000 miles/year). Now we need to multiply that figure by three hundred million (300,000,000) light years. That's the distance across the universe, at least that we are currently aware of. When we multiply those two figures together, we finally get the physical dimension of how much God loves us. Which is one quintillion, seventy seven quadrillion miles. Here is the actual numerical figure (1,770,000,000,000,000,000 miles). When God holds out his hands and says, "I love you this much!" His hands would spread apart until they reached this distance of one quintillion, seventy seven quadrillion miles. **Do you know how far that distance is? If you did, it would revolutionize your perspective of God's love and it would change you instantly, drastically and constantly. God wants us to have a mind blowing, supernatural, radiant revelation of his love towards us.**

Sometimes God reveals himself to us in layers as we draw closer to him and sometimes God's love is like trying to take a drink from the Niagara Falls by standing under it with your mouth open. Either way is fine because both revelations are going to transform your life. As you begin to have a deeper understanding of how much God loves you, it will exponentially magnify how you love God, yourself and finally others. God says his children are to shine like the noonday sun and we are to be a light of love in this dark world.

God doesn't want you to doubt his love for one moment. When you understand his love, it will change everything about you, your world and the people around you. God's love will change how you think, talk and act. It will change how hard you laugh. It will change your perspective on life and your relationships with people. It will give you the patience you so desperately need while serving and caring for people.

I dare you to try to love God back as much as he loves you. Of course it's not possible but he'd love for you to try. All of your life is about trying to do just that. **God tells us that loving him is the greatest thing you will ever do with your life.** Jesus said this is the first and greatest commandment:

You should love the Lord with <u>ALL</u> your heart,
with <u>ALL</u> your soul and with <u>ALL</u> your mind.
Matthew 22:37

God is patiently waiting for us to fall head over heels in love with him. Partial commitment means you haven't had a complete revelation of his love. God desires complete surrender with all our heart, mind and soul. **He has so much information to give us about himself, it's going to take one hundred percent of our heart, mind, soul & life to absorb it all!** God wants us to radiate with all his many character attributes as we walk out into the world and shine the light of his glory. I know for a fact how much God loves me. He's revealed it to me in so many unique and profound ways. The great news is, God loves you just as much as he loves me. The best kept secret in the whole world is this:

God loves people!

Most of the world doesn't understand the depth of that statement. People don't know it, they refuse to comprehend it and they never receive it. People think they have to earn God's love through behavior modification, but you can't. It's something given freely for everyone to receive. Even most of the Christian community believes you have to do certain things or act a certain way for God to love you. **God is not going to love you any better when you become better. He is not going to love you more when you do more good things for him.** You just can't stop God from loving you, but you can refuse to receive it or limit it. You can run from God and turn your back on his love. Remember you don't have to act a certain way for God to love you. Otherwise he wouldn't love any of us. The bible says:

God proved he loved us, because EVEN WHILE WE WERE SINNERS, Christ died for us. Romans 5:8

Why did God love us if we are all a bunch of rebellious, wayward, God rejecting, self-centered sinners? **Because God's love is not dictated by our actions.** God's love is sometimes difficult to describe to people. It has to be experienced, like standing at the edge of the Grand Canyon. God's love is not controlled by evil. When we are disobedient, we will have repercussions for those actions because it gives Satan an inroad to our lives (Romans 6:16). But God's love for us is a constant force that surrounds us. **His love in our spirit is a catalyst for experiencing life and peace. Romans 8:6**

A greater understanding of how much God loves you will drastically accelerate your maturity level. This supernatural love from God is the catalyst of our Christian character. A catalyst is defined as a substance introduced into a process that modifies and exponentially increases the rate of change of the reaction. What a great word to describe God's love for us, IT'S A CATALYST!

God's love is the substance, that is introduced into the process of our lives, that exponentially increases the rate of how much we forgive, prefer and serve one another. God's love is a catalyst and it causes a chain-reaction in us.

<u>To experience God's love in its greatest capacity:</u>

We need to READ about God's love.

We need to LEARN about God's love.

We need to UNDERSTAND how much God loves us.

We need to RECEIVE God's love with all our heart.

Don't reject it, turn from it or limit it.

We need to MEDITATE on the
love of God throughout the day.

We need to RECIPROCATE God's love.

Love him back with the love he gave you.

We need to GIVE God's love to others.
(Freely, unrestricted, unmerited and unconditional)

Jesus said the greatest thing you could ever do is:

Love the Lord with all your heart, with all your soul, with all your mind and with all your strength. Mark 12:30

The second greatest thing you could ever do, once you understand and are doing the first thing is this:

Love your neighbor like their one of your own family members. Matthew 22:39

If you ever wondered what God's will is for your life, it is all right there. God's love is the catalyst for being in his will.

Build yourselves up in your most holy faith by praying in the Holy Spirit and keep yourselves immersed in God's love. Jude 1:20 & 21

Today child of God, draw a line in the sand, go and write it on a wooden stake then drive it into the ground on your property. Write it on the walls of your house, write it on your clothes or on the bottom of your shoes with a permanent marker and pronounce to him:

TODAY GOD...I RECEIVE
THE FULLNESS OF YOUR LOVE.

Your interpretation of God's loving nature towards you, is the most important thought you'll ever have.

Now God can operate in that type of faith, passion and surrender. That's what he's been waiting for. God wants people to receive him into their spirit and then release him out of their spirit for others to experience. I've observed that many people, to various degrees, have built up walls around themselves to keep others at a safe distance. This seems to be an instinctive defensive mechanism built within people so that they don't get hurt. **God's love will rip apart every wall you've built, the moment you crack open the door to him.** He will fill that box you've created around yourself with so much of his love that soon it will burst wide open. LEARN about God's love, RECEIVE his love, ACCEPT it, MEDITATE on it daily, be CONFIDENT of it, be SECURE in it and TRUST in his love.

STORY – Love Letter

One time I was driving to work early in the morning. It was dark and raining which made it extremely difficult to see. There in my car, I was talking to God and letting him know that I felt like he was a thousand miles away from me. I wasn't feeling him close to me like other days. So I asked God a stupid question, I said, "God do you really love me?" There was a ten second pause from Heaven. Then a semi-truck came speeding by very fast. As the back end of the truck went by, I notice in the lower right corner of the truck, there were three words written there. Someone used their fingertip to write these words on that dirty truck:

GOD LOVES YOU.

I thought to myself, WHAT! WHAT just happened here! God...is that you! Did you just write me a note on the back of that semi-truck? Did you have someone write it earlier and then time the truck to go by right when I needed to see that? Was it just a coincidence that I happened to be asking that question to you and then this truck went by at the exact time I needed to hear from you?

Instead of questioning God's response and asking him why he would ever take the time to ever love someone like me. I just decided to receive those three words that God had written to me and allow the truth to penetrate into my heart. GOD LOVES ME! It might as well have said:

GOD LOVES YOU ERIC DEAN JOHNSON

...

17

...because that's how I received it. My heart started filling up at that moment with the love of God. I couldn't understand what was happening to me. I was just completely overwhelmed with the power, presence and love of God. I started crying with tears of joy, receiving and understanding God's love in a marvelous and profound way.

Maybe you've been down that same road I was on that morning. I think we all have. We all have those days when we just don't feel like God is close. I want you to start a new habit. I want you to say this when you first open your eyes in the morning.

GOD LOVES ME and I LOVE HIM and
I'M GOING TO GO and LOVE OTHERS.

God has his arms spread open wide to the people of this world and he's saying to them, "I LOVE YOU...I CREATED YOU...YOU ARE MINE." We struggle, push away and run from the very thing that we so desperately need....THE LOVE OF GOD IN OUR HEARTS.

God is trying to capture the world's attention,
look into their eyes and say...I LOVE YOU.
Those who surrender to him and receive it...
WILL BE CHANGED FOREVER.

LOVE PEOPLE

Love each other deeply from your heart.
I Peter 1:22

Don't get tired of blessing and helping people. For in time you shall receive a great reward for your faith-filled words and actions. So take advantage of every opportunity in reflecting Christ's love towards others. Galatians 6:9 & 10

Be completely humble, gentle and patient when loving one another, because you are united in God's love through his Holy Spirit. Ephesians 4:2 & 3

God wants us to love one another because GOD IS LOVE and that's how we perfectly resemble him. Have you ever noticed the statements parents make when they see their new born baby for the first time? They say things like, "He has your eyes, she has your nose or he has your chin." We're anxious to see the resemblances of our children in us. In the exact same way God is waiting to see how we resemble him. Not with our nose, chin and eyes but with *our spirit.* **In our born-again spirit we're identical to God. He intertwined his spirit around our new spirit and now we're united with him (I Corinthians 6:16).** Our thoughts and actions are not identical to God's because were all in *the process* of learning about this love that's in our spirit. As we learn and mature we begin to love like he does. **God wants us to love and forgive like no one else on the earth. He wants us to express his character traits for the entire world to see.**

The world will chase after that type of love, if we would just extend it to them. We'll be able to look them straight in the eye and tell them, "GOD LOVES YOU", and they will finally begin to believe it. Then we'll be able to share with them the hope that we have in the Lord. We'll be able to share with them the gospel message of the Lord Jesus Christ in a way they will understand, believe and receive. That's the whole point of Christianity. God is reaching out TO YOU (his child) and then he reaches out THROUGH YOU (to others).

Religion is all about people trying to reach God through strict performance based works, rituals and doctrines. New Testament Christianity is about God reaching out to his children through love, mercy and grace.

God is very specific on how we are to treat people. He continually tells us in his word to love others because that's how we resemble Christ. When your relationship with God grows deeper then your relationships with others will change as well. Your overwhelming love and compassion for others will be the evidence to them that you are a child of God.

When we completely understand and totally receive God's love, then we will be able to love others with that same unconditional love, regardless of how they treat us. That's what the word *unconditional* means; there's no strings attached, no requirements to fulfill and no list of conditions to meet. The love I have for other people comes from an overflowing source in me, put there by God. God is passionate about people and that same passion was deposited in our spirit when we were born-again. God's love should flow through us regardless of how we're treated or how others respond to us or even whether they choose to love us back.

Is your love for others based on their performance or is it based on the new nature that's in you. God's love in us causes us to hope for the best in people. We shouldn't look for the worst in them; the rest of the world is doing that. If you can't seem to find anything good in a particular person, then hope to see the best in them one day. God's love in us always hopes to make a tremendous impact on others.

God is love and love overflows with hope.
God _hopes_ that people will turn
from their wicked ways.
God _hopes_ that people will love him back.
God _hopes_ that his creation will humble themselves
before him. God _hopes_ that we will seek his face,
understand his nature and know him completely.
God _hopes_ for and envies our prayers.

STORY – Love Hopes For The Best

One time I made this collage of three pictures in a frame for my wife. The first picture was of her and I hugging together under a waterfall in Jamaica on our honeymoon. The scripture verse I put under that picture was from Proverbs 12:4 it says, *"A wife of noble character is her husband's crown."* The second one was a picture of our two daughters. The verse under that picture said, *"Her children will rise up and call her blessed."* The third picture was a beautiful photo of her and under that picture I put a scripture from Proverbs 31, *"She is clothed with strength and dignity. She speaks with wisdom and faithful instructions are on her lips. A woman who loves the Lord is a valuable treasure to find."*

When I first made this frame for her, those scriptures were a hope that I had for my wife one day. I held on to those scriptures and prayed them over her. I believed that my wife was going to be a Proverbs 31 woman one day. Today, all these many years later, the things I had hoped for have come to pass. My wife loves the Lord more than anyone else I know. She is a woman of noble character. She is clothed with strength and integrity.

Hope is a powerful thing. Many times hope is all we have to hold onto in life. **Hope is an attribute that we should mix with our faith, prayers and praise.** Hope is something we need to cling to and embrace everyday. Don't ever give up on anyone. Hope and pray for them. Hope for the best in people by loving them God's way.

LOVING PEOPLE GOD'S WAY

I try to be the most difficult person to offend. I try not to be easily provoked or angered. Sometimes I'm successful at it and sometimes I'm not. It depends on how much time I've spent renewing my mind in God's word and understanding that his character attributes have been placed in my spirit. **God's love enables us to repel the offenses that come our way.** One time someone told me that another person said something against me. I could have thought to myself:

I knew that person didn't like me.
I'll get back at them some way.
I'll never talk to them again.

Instead, I told that person I was talking to, "No, they would have never said that about me. They must have meant something different. You must have misunderstood them or they probably didn't mean it the way you interpreted it." You see love hopes for the best in people, not the worst. God's love in us doesn't latch on to the negative but always hopes for a positive outcome.

If we would just love others the way God loves us...
the world would drastically change overnight.

God has supernaturally channeled his love into our hearts through his Holy Spirit (Romans 5:5). As we discover more about this love that God has placed in our spirit, then we'll be able to shower others with it at tremendous levels. The world desperately needs a mighty revelation of God's true nature towards them.

STORY: A Kind Word

One afternoon as my wife's hospital shift was beginning, many of her co-workers told her about this extremely irritable and angry patient. No one went into his room unless it was absolutely necessary. Everyone knowing my wife's personality, knew she was completely up for the challenge. As soon as she went into this man's room he began barking at her constantly about everything. He insulted her and complained about everything and everyone.

But it was all to no avail, it was like rain dripping off a ducks back. My wife didn't allow his words to penetrate her, but her words did penetrate him. She was soft spoken and cordial. She got him some ice water and repositioned him so he was more comfortable. She showed him genuine care, concern and loved him with words and actions.

The other nurses were surprised that she was in his room for so long. They thought, "What was going on in there? Was he strangling her to death?" They didn't hear any yelling from the room any more. Finally, as she was coming out of the room, she turned and joked with the guy about something and the both laughed. The other nurses stood in amazement.

What had just happened in there?

My wife was displaying some biblical principles that never fail. A few scriptures that come to mind for this situation are.

A soft word diffuses a person's anger. Proverbs 15:1

Prefer one another above yourself. Romans 12:10

Love your neighbor like they're the most important person in the world to you. Matthew 22:39

Be kind and compassionate to everyone. Ephesians 4:32

Don't be overcome by evil thoughts, but overcome evil with the love that's in your spirit. Romans 12:21

No weapon formed against you will ever succeed. Isaiah 54:17

Don't let any unwholesome words come out of your mouth but only speak words that are encouraging for others to hear. Ephesians 4:29

The patient was hateful, abusive and offensive. He spent most of the day cursing at everyone. But God's love was flowing out of my wife's spirit; she was loving, patient, kind and compassionate. **The love of God drastically transforms people; don't subdue it, UNLEASH IT ON OTHERS!** It will change all of your relationships around you. God's love drastically changes how you think and respond to people. When you love people with the love of the Lord, you always hope for the best in others. Love disarms angry, frustrated, hurting people. It melts away those icy walls people build up around themselves. Love confuses and disarms our enemies (Proverbs 16:7). God's love will cast out that fear in you. His love in you will cause you to be patient, persevere and prevail. I Corinthians 13:7

You can only get as close to God…
as the person you love the least.

25

I just love the wisdom behind that statement. You might want to read that sentence over and over until you completely understand it. God wants us to love people; he wants his love multiplied exponentially over the earth through us! There is a whole world of people out there to love and God wants us to go and *love them all!* It's going to take some of your time, energy and maybe even a little bit of money. You may also have to give up some sleep, but it will be worth it. **A life filled with loving people is a fulfilled, satisfying, successful and blessed life.**

We're not allowed to choose who we're going to love and who we're not going to love. We're not allowed to choose who we're going to forgive and who we're not going to forgive. Born-again Christians love people, they don't know any other way. It's ingrained in their *new nature* of being IN CHRIST. Blood bought, Holy Spirit filled Christians forgive people no matter what the offense. Forgiveness is not a choice we make, it's actually a part of our new nature. **Christians, who unconditionally forgive, clearly understand the debt of the sin that they have been forgiven of. Forgiveness is attached to our identity.** Forgiveness has become a part of who we are. It's not only something we do but it's a character attribute of our divinely filled spirit.

Christians are forgiving people…
because we are forgiven people.

It seems like the bible is always teaching us to respond to others contrary to how the world responds. For example:

If your enemy is hungry, feed him. Romans 12:20
If you love those who only love you, what good is that?
Matthew 5:46
If someone strikes you on the cheek, turn to him the other cheek. Matthew 5:39
If someone takes your cloak give him your tunic also.
Matthew 5:40

Jesus said, "Love your enemies and bless those who curse you, do good to people who hate you and pray for people who despitefully use you and persecute you."
Matthew 5:44

Do you see what I mean? The wisdom of God is completely different from the wisdom of this world. **When you overwhelm people with love, you are revealing to them the heart of God.** Does God's love flow out of your heart like a river or does it drip from your tight lips like a leaky faucet? Let love flow out of your heart like a mighty flood, pushing forward, rising higher and moving into new areas. God's love is like a waterfall from Heaven which lands on us and spills out over into the community.

The bible has a lot to say about loving people God's way. The word love is mentioned over eight hundred times in the bible. Extending people the love of God is a privilege and something they will not soon forget. **The love of Christ coming out of you will challenge every emotion in you.** God's love is always *others*-centered and never *self*-centered.

Maybe you just can't love people that way. You just don't feel like you have it in you. How are you going to love people with this type of love? You're going to need some help. You won't know how to love many of the difficult people in your life, but the Holy Spirit will show you how.

God has poured out his love into our hearts by the Holy Spirit whom he has given us. Romans 5:5

I will send you the Holy Spirit and he will endue you with power from the high Heavens. Luke 24:49

The Holy Spirit will show you how to love these hurting, dysfunctional, frustrated, difficult people in the world. **Remember, hurting people hurt other people.** You can't go by your feelings when loving people, you have to go by what God says from his word through your spirit. We have to respond with spiritual wisdom to the world's condition. **When people hurt you don't take it personal. They just don't know how to love others the way you do. The enemy wants you to be offended but God wants you to be a peace maker.** God can heal that broken, hurting person that is so difficult for you to love.

What good is it if you only love those who love you? Even a hateful person can do that! Matthew 5:46

God wants you to be different when it comes to loving difficult people, because you are different. God wants you to love people like no one else on the planet, because you are like no one else on the planet.

STORY – The Hand Shake Song

Every Sunday in our church we have what is called "The Hand Shake Song". It's a time when you get out of your seat and go around and shake hands with everyone, hug them or give someone an encouraging word. We also get to meet new visitors at this time and fellowship with each other for a few minutes while a song is being played. One time God spoke to me just before "The Hand Shake Song" and I'll never forget what he said to me:

"Go and love my people for me. They don't understand how much I love them and I want to channel MY LOVE THROUGH YOU TO THEM. I can see that you have my spirit working in you and that you'll allow me to love them through you. Go and love every one of them for me."

WOW! What an awesome word from God! Now every Sunday just before "The Hand Shake Song" I hear those words ring out from my spirit, "GO AND LOVE THEM ALL." That crystal clear message that God spoke to me that day, is actually for all of God's children.

We're all striving to be vessels that God can flow through and loving others is an important part of that process. **God wants us to allow Christ (who lives in us) to express himself outwardly towards others, through our personalities, emotions, thoughts, words and actions.** If you always allow him to do that, then you will always be in the will of God. You will be fulfilled, complete and happy. You'll be content and at peace as Christ comes out of you. **Trust the person of Christ who lives in you and enjoy his accomplishments as he comes out of you through your words and actions.**

<u>I've heard a lot of people say:</u>

You don't know my neighbor. It would be scary to go over there and try to make amends with them. I don't know how they would respond to me. You don't know what my spouse did to me. That pain would be too much for me to confront again. You don't know what my angry child said to me when they ran out that door.

I'm afraid to make the first move.
I'm afraid of being rejected.
I'm afraid they might hurt me again.
I'm afraid they won't love me back.

<u>Here is what the Lord would say to that fear inside of you:</u>

MY perfect LOVE casts out fear.
MY LOVE damages fear.
MY LOVE crushes fear.
MY LOVE breaks the yoke of fear.
MY LOVE triumphs over fear.
MY LOVE melts away fear.
(I John 4:16-18)

So take a step of faith and trust God. He's all about restoring broken relationships. When we trust God and take those steps of love, then he will come sweeping into our situation with his ministering spirit. He will soften and change those hard hearts around you. God's love melts away the cold, icy heart.

God is depending on us to share his message
of reconciliation between himself and mankind.
II Corinthians 5:19

STORY - Never Fight With A Red-Headed Woman

I remember one time my wife and I were fighting about something stupid. She was mad, frustrated and yelling at me. Usually I'm very patient, but this time I was fighting back just as hard. Then I got a revelation from God.

"Go to her, put your arms around her and just look into her eyes until she sees how much you love her. Nothing else matters more to her than that, and don't let go of her, no matter what she says".

Now that's a dangerous thing to do to a mad, red-headed woman. So I did exactly that. I did exactly as the Holy Spirit instructed me. She fought back and struggled to get away from me, but after a few minutes, we were laughing, loving and forgiving. GOD'S LOVE MELTS HEARTS, it really does.

God's love comforts the offended heart.
God's love fills the empty heart.
God's love heals the broken heart.
God's love heals the unforgiving heart.
God's love heals the abandoned heart.

My wife and I could have stayed angry at each other. We could have gone to bed mad. We could have allowed that anger to grow deeper and fester into hatred, rage and bitterness. We could have allowed our household to be a place of division and strife. We could have gotten a divorce and in the end we would have learned absolutely nothing about the supernatural, unconditional, never ending love of God.

Be completely humble, gentle and patient when loving one another. Make every effort to keep the unity of the Spirit through the bond of peace. Ephesians 4:2 & 3

When the world sees your good works emulating from God's love, they will glorify your Father in Heaven.
I Peter 2:12

God wants the world to look at his children, full, complete and operating in his love and say, "WOW...that's completely different from anything I've seen in a long time! I WANT THAT! I want to know them and what they're all about." **People are drawn to God's love, not rules, doctrines and church protocol.** There's not a person that has ever lived, that wanted to be unloved and unaccepted. People want to be loved, accepted and valued. Let the Holy Spirit soften their hard heart, that's what he specializes in (John 16:8). Our responsibility is to extend to people the love of God because we are ministers of reconciliation. You might be thinking:

Lord...it will be difficult to love everyone with the same unrestricted and unconditional love. How do I love people like this? This is a love I don't fully understand. It's a love that I never really expressed before. But Lord, I WANT IT! I want to know how to love others the way you love me.

It's that kind of hunger and desire that releases God's love from our spirit. God says his love for us is higher than the Heavens are above the earth. That means we can search out all the many facets of God's love for the rest of our lives and continually discover all the many unique ways that he loves us. God's love is so vast; it's hard to fully comprehend, but WE ALL SO DESPERATELY NEED IT. All of his creation longs for it because God designed us that way.

God has already placed his love in our spirit, but we are the ones who regulate the unraveling process of his love. We determine everyday the speed at which we want to learn about his love and express his love. God's love knows no limits...so don't limit it.

When God supernaturally fills you up and you begin to understand the extreme depth of his love, then you can't help but let it flow out to others. You'll love that difficult boss, or your distant spouse, that frustrated neighbor or that impossible teenager. It won't be through your own strength, it will be God operating through you.

GOD WILL SURPRISE YOU WITH THE NEW

When we became born-again Christians, we were given the Spirit of God to live on the *inside of us* so that Christ could come alive on the *outside of us* through our thoughts, attitude, words and actions. The spirit of Christ literally lives in us (Romans 8:9). Our old sin nature was completely pulverized and obliterated the moment Christ moved in. Our old spirit is now dead and our new spirit is dancing with new supernatural life. That's an incredible source of power we have in us. Our fleshly desires (that were driven by our old nature) are in the process of dieing, but we are dead to sin in our spirit (Romans 6:2,6,7,11). **The fleshly desires we have now are the residual effects of old thought patterns and habits. They will try to influence you when you meditate on them. How much time you spend thinking about the OLD self versus the NEW you, will determine how much victory you have over the flesh.** That's why it's important to keep learning about the NEW spirit that's in you. Don't ever forget that you're a child of the King. In the spirit realm you wear a royal robe, a beautiful crown, a gold ring and you carry a dazzling scepter.

Our old sinful nature was crucified with Christ.
It was destroyed so that we no longer have
to serve it as our master. Romans 6:6

Born-again Christians are taught and lead by a completely new nature. The Holy Spirit wants to break out of your soul like a run away freight train and release that new fruit that's in you. It's going to completely surprise your old way of thinking. The bi-product (fruit) of being filled with the Holy Spirit is love, peace, joy, gentleness, patience, kindness, goodness, faithfulness and self-control. God has already given us all the patience, peace, joy and love that we will ever need for this life. It's there deep down inside of us. How did it get there? It was transferred there through the Holy Spirit when you accepted Christ as Lord of your life. **You are now IN CHRIST and since Christ is not lacking in any of these attributes, then we also have all that we need for an abundant life and victorious living.** We just need to let that love, peace, patience and joy flow out of our spirit and into our mind, soul, mouth and actions. Your spirit has been touched by God. Your spirit is now alive, alert and in hot pursuit of God's desires. You literally have the life of God within you. You are a completely new creation IN-CHRIST. So get ready for a life filled with many new and exciting surprises.

All the different fruits of the Spirit that Galatians 5:22 & 23 speak of are the character attributes of God. They may not be something you understand completely. They are character attributes that come out of your new born-again spirit. The Holy Spirit will challenge you to respond to people or a situation with this new spirit that lives in you.

We Christians must rely on the Holy Spirit to lead us, counsel us and teach us. If we harden our hearts to his voice, then we cannot be empowered by him. In essence we would be saying to God, "Thanks for saving me, but I'll take over from here and guide myself through this Christian life". That would be crazy! You don't have a clue about what a divine and holy God could want from you.

Those who are in the flesh can not please God.
Romans 8:8

Don't be fooled by the enemy, the work that God started in you through his spirit, cannot be completed by trying to perceive spiritual things through you carnal flesh.
Galatians 3:3

We don't help the Holy Spirit the Holy Spirit helps us. You could read the bible and put your own spin on it. You could try to discern it for yourself, but that would lead to all kinds of trouble. Who knows the mind of Christ except the Spirit of God (I Corinthians 2:16). **The Holy Spirit helps us read and interpret the truth in God's word. We need the Holy Spirit to translate, decipher and filter everything we see, think, feel, experience and say in life.**

One of the bookmarkers I've complied is called *WHAT ARE WE TO DO WITH ONE ANOTHER*. It tells us how we are to treat one another. It explains what God's love in us will accomplish in our relationships around us.

WHAT ARE WE TO DO
WITH ONE ANOTHER?

Be DEVOTED to one another in LOVE.
We are to ENCOURAGE one another.
We are to FORGIVE each other.
We are to REJOICE with one another.
We are to PRAY for one another.
We are to EXHORT one another.
We are to SHINE THE LIGHT to one another.
We are to be PATIENT with one another.
We are to be KIND to one another.
We are to be GENTLE towards one another.
We are to STAND FIRM with one another.
We are to be LIKE MINDED with each other.
We are to extend FAVOR to one another.
We are to CELEBRATE one another.
We are to CARE for one another.
We are to HOPE with one another.
We are to BELIEVE with one another.
We are to be GENEROUS with one another.
We are to LOOK FOR THE BEST in each other.
We are to BEAR one another's burdens.
Be COMPASSIONATE to one another.
We are to HONOR one another.
Be THANKFUL for one another.
Live in HARMONY with one another.
ACCEPT and GREET one another.
We are to be UNITED with one another.
We are to SERVE one another in love.
Offer HOSPITALITY to one another.
We are to FELLOWSHIP with one another.

complied by Eric Johnson

SELF-CENTERED TO CHRIST-CENTERED
TO OTHERS-CENTERED

God is passionate about restoring the relationship between you and him. He is also passionate about restoring relationships between you and your family, friends and anyone else in your circle of fellowship. Why, because you are his ambassador (II Corinthians 5:20). You are his representative here on this earth. **God wants to manifest his divine character attributes through you. How you act will determine what people think about the God that you love, serve and promote.**

You should live in harmony with one another.
Be sympathetic, compassionate and humble.
Live together like a closely knit family does. Do not repay evil with evil or insult with insult, but shower each other with compliments, encouraging words and blessings. You have been called to live a triumphant, exhilarating and blessed life. I Peter 3:8 & 9

Children of God, there are so many things we can glean from that one scripture. God knows what he's talking about. The bible is not God's self-help book so that we can improve our life and have better relationships. First God wants us redeemed and reconciled to him, then he wants us to reflect the light of his truth and character to others. This is challenging stuff he wants to accomplish in our lives. **There is spiritual warfare taking place every time you think a thought and every time you open your mouth.** Will it be blessings or cursing, will it be life or death? Will it be a positive thought or a negative word?

I have set before you life and death, blessing and cursing. I hope that you will choose life so that you and your family may prosper. Deuteronomy 30:19

You can change your family's future not only by the words you speak but also by the thoughts you think. You can sever those muti-generational curses by the choices and changes you make in your life today.

I Peter 3:8 & 9 is a clear promise from God. If you *do* what it says, you will *receive* what it promises. God cannot and will not back down on a promise. So if we love, live in harmony and be peace makers, then you'll walk in God's blessings all day long. Maybe you have some difficult people to love around you. WELCOME TO EARTH! Here is some good news. **God has put the fullness of his nature in you, to teach you everything you need to know about him.**

Loving difficult people is…DIFFICULT!
But God commands us to love them,
so you know his Holy Spirit will show us how.

This is how we know what love is: Jesus Christ laid down his life for us and we ought to lay down our lives for each other. If anyone has material possessions and sees someone in need but has no pity on them, how can the love of God be in them? Dear children, let us not love with words only but with actions propelled by God's Spirit in us. I John 3:16-18

As God's love touches your spirit it will burst from your heart and flow out to others. Everyone who loves unconditionally without restraint has had a deep, inner heart transforming experience with the love of God.
I John 4:7 & 8

Anyone who understands that the fullness of God's love lives in their spirit, will be able to love others beyond their own inner strength. I John 4:21

STORY – *Loving Others With Actions*

The Northeast Blackout of 2003 was a massive widespread power outage that occurred throughout parts of the Northeastern and Midwestern United States and Ontario, Canada on Thursday, August 14, 2003. The blackout affected an estimated 10 million people in Ontario and 45 million people in eight U.S. states. At the time, it was the second most widespread electrical blackout in history.

My neighbors were all outside talking about it when I got home from work. It was also devastating to hear that none of the gas stations could pump any gas. My daughter called me and said her best friend's mom was completely out of gas and needed help. I had a full five gallons in the garage so I drove over to her house and gave her some. For just a moment when I was pouring gas into her car, some thoughts came to my mind.

You might need some of this gas later for
your own car or maybe for your generator.
This is a major multi-state power outage.
You don't know how long you're going to be without
power. You better keep your gas to yourself.

Then the word of the Lord came to me:

If anyone has material possessions and sees his neighbor in need, but has no pity on them, how can the love of God be in them? I John 3:17

So I aligned my thinking with the word of God. I said, "God is going to take care of me. I am not going to be without anything he wants me to have." Yes, this was a fearful time with many questions in my mind. But my faith and love are going to move forward and trust God. I serve a God who has an unlimited supply of resources. The more I pour out to people in need (love and gas), the more God can refill my supply. My faith was tested soon after that when my wife called me and said her friend at work had absolutely no gas and she had a forty minute drive home, could I come and help. I said, "Of course," and immediately went and gave her some gas.

Here is a word of wisdom about maturity. What God freely gives us; we should freely extend to others. That's why God gave it to us. God loves us and wants us to love others with our time, money, words, thoughts and actions. God has forgiven us and wants us to extend forgiveness to others (Ephesians 4:32). God has blessed us and wants us to be a blessing to others. God has many divine attributes that he has lavished on us and he wants us to operate in those gifts.

Freely you have received...so freely give.
Matthew 10:8

STORY – *God Will Supply All My Needs*

Our Church owns a campground out in the middle of the country. It's about forty miles from my house. I was going to drive to the youth camp meetings all that week and I knew it would probably take an entire tank of gas to drive out there all week long. I only had about a quarter tank of gas and I was concerned about it. I began to just talk to God out loud and I said,

"Lord...I want to minister to these youths who have come out here to this revival. I'm here to pray for them, speak faith-filled words over them and encourage them. I'm here to serve you in any way I can. I'm not going to let my gas gauge distract me from my purpose. I'm doing the little things that I know how to do and I need you to come in and do the big things that you can most certainly do. My trust is in you completely. In-fact, I believe right now, as I actually touch my finger to the instrument panel and put it over the gas gauge, you can fill my tank up with gas."

WOW...that's pretty crazy! Maybe I shouldn't be doing this? Isn't this challenging God? I mean should I really expect God to fill my gas tank? Isn't my gas tank my own responsibility? But the Holy Spirit rose up in me and said,

Move your finger to the full line on the gas gauge.

Was God going to fill my gas tank right before my eyes? Maybe it was just my own voice in my head, challenging God for a miracle. Was I letting my emotions get ahead of my faith? Isn't this border-line fanatical?

Then I heard that same voice again rise up in my spirit.

Move your finger to the full line on the gas gauge.

I began to slide my finger from the quarter tank of gas mark to the full line. I did it over and over as if God was actually going to supernaturally fill my gas tank. I **didn't just obey what the Holy Spirit said, but I believed what the Holy Spirit said.** Did God fill my tank? NO! What happened? Didn't I have enough faith? Then God's word leaped out of my spirit:

God will liberally supply every one of my needs according to his glorious riches obtained for us through Christ Jesus. Philippians 4:19

I started laughing at my gas gauge. I thought to myself, this gas issue is a very little thing in God's eyes. If I can't trust God for a simple tank of gas, how am I going to trust him to miraculously transform these young people who I'm going to pray for tonight? How am I going to trust God to supernaturally intervene in the lives of these young people if I couldn't even trust him to get me there?

The gas wasn't the priority prayer for the moment. Those young people were who I should be concerned about. Salvation and souls were what I should be focused on. I needed to focus my prayer on the bigger things that God was planning on doing that night in the lives of people. I was not going to do without anything God needed me to have, THAT'S A SUPERNATURAL FACT! **God is going to supply all of my needs because he promised he would and his promises are more real to me than a gas needle that's moving towards empty or anything in this life.**

We had a phenomenal service that night. God moved in ways that I'll never forget. Lives were touched and broken hearts were healed. God filled the entire sanctuary with his love and presence that night.

Did God move my gas needle from EMPTY to FULL? NO! Did I have the faith that he could do it? YES! Did I get down and disappointed when God didn't supply all my needs? NO! I walked by faith and not by sight (II Corinthians 5:7). God said it...so I believe it! I believed that my car could run on empty for as long as I needed it to. That may sound silly to a lot of you...but not me. Even as I saw that gas needle move farther and father towards empty...I STAYED IN FAITH.

The very next day, someone at church handed me cash to specifically go and fill up MY GAS TANK!

I never even said anything to that person about gas, being low on gas or not having any money for gas. How did this happen? Because of a promise God made to me.

My child, you can trust me to supply all your needs, based on my compassion, love and my promises.
Philippians 4:19

God saw!
God cares!
God loves!
God supplies!
God is in control of it all!
God is worthy to be praised!

I guarantee if there would have been other people in my car and I would have put my finger on my gas gauge and said, "God fill it up!" They would have laughed me right out of the car, maybe even if they were Christians. **I don't know how God is going to accomplish everything he promised us. It's not my job to figure it**

all out. My responsibility is to step out in faith, not doubt and believe that God will be faithful to his promises.

In Matthew 9:23 a little girl had DIED and Jesus still went to visit her. We are talking no heart beat, no blood flow and no breathing. SHE WAS DEAD! Someone ran to tell Jesus not to bother coming to the house, the GIRL WAS DEAD! The people at her house were wailing and mourning over her because SHE WAS DEAD! When Jesus reached her house, he told them, *"She isn't dead, she's only sleeping."* The crowd must have thought he was crazy because they knew SHE WAS DEAD! There was a lot of DEAD TALK going around that day. Every word that came out of these people's mouths regarding this girl was about DEATH. But ETERNAL LIFE walked right through the crowd of DEATH. The giver of LIFE stepped into the house of DEATH. The people knew all about DEATH, they recognized it and they lived around it. That's why they didn't recognize THE AUTHOR OF LIFE.

Jesus said, "I am the resurrection and the life, anyone who believes in me, even if they were to die, will live with me forever." John 11:25

Do you know how many dead people Jesus has raised to LIFE? Do you know how many dead spirits Jesus has touched and they leaped to life? The answer is...ALL OF THEM! That's his specialty. When he touches people their spirit leaps. Every dead person (dead in their spirit) that looks to Jesus Christ and says:

I believe you are the Son of God.
I believe you died for my sins.
I believe you rose from the grave.
I receive your salvation into my spirit...

...are RAISED FROM THE DEAD
in their spirit through Christ.

Before we got saved, we were as dead as dead can be (in our spirit). But now we have been raised up from the dead, in a similar and supernatural way that Christ was resurrected.

A lot of people believe that God doesn't speak to people today like he used to. They believe God has already said everything he's going to say. A lot of people believe that God doesn't perform miracles today, like he's been doing ever since the beginning of time. I just laugh when I hear people who believe that way. They just haven't discovered God in his deepest dimension. **God reveals himself to people who trust him, believe in him, obey him and release him out of their spirit through faith. Faith is how God's nature and purpose are promoted and glorified on the earth.**

Don't hinder the flow of God's miracle working power in your life. We get into trouble when we stop the flow of God's love, mercy, grace and forgiveness. When we choose not to extend the forgiveness that was so freely extended to us, then we get ourselves into complete disarray and turmoil in the spiritual realm. It's in those key moments that we will either do one of two things. We will either give the enemy a foothold in our lives or we will release God's glory from our spirit. There's NO POWER when there's NO FORGIVENESS. There's NO POWER when there's NO LOVE. There's NO POWER when there's NO HOPE. Christians need to keep the free flowing river of God's attributes moving and operating in their lives. **God's character attributes were deposited in us so they could flow out of us.**

Forgive...just as God has completely forgiven you.
Ephesians 4:32

The love of the Lord is unlimited...so don't limit it. Don't get yourself in the position where you hinder the free flowing attributes of God's character in your life. By limiting the outflow of Godly character to others you limit your ability to mature in Christ and grow towards your destiny. Understanding your identity IN CHRIST is directly connected with your maturity and purpose. God has filled you with his love so you can go and release it on others.

If you want unlimited growth, wisdom, power, anointing and peace in your life; then don't interrupt the flow of God's love, forgiveness, compassion, mercy and grace towards others.

Surrender to the Holy Spirit as he prompts you to love, forgive, help, encourage, listen to and understand people. How you treat others is an indicator of how much you've renewed your mind. **God will inject health and healing into your relationships when you love people beyond your own capabilities and extend to them God's grace, mercy and love from within your spirit.** I've seen and experienced disappointing behavior from Christians in my life. That must be extremely painful for God also. When we don't understand God's love in its fullness, then we will fail and fall more often. **God has a spectacular life planned for us to experience and it begins immediately as we understand what his divine nature in us is capable of.**

We have the supernatural presence of our divine God IN US. God himself, through the person of Christ, resides within us. Just BE YOU...BE IN CHRIST. Christians make being a Christian so much more difficult than it really is. We are IN CHRIST. That means we now want what he wants and that's how Christians find true fulfillment. It comes by expressing and letting the life of Christ come out of us.

God is passionate about you! Are you just as passionate about him? He longs to hear from us. He wants to hear your voice and look into your eyes. He watches you when you sleep at night. His thoughts about us are too numerous to count. When we finally *get it* and truly understand God's love, then we'll be able to *give it* to others unconditionally. For some of you it will take a lifetime to understand God's divine character, the fullness of his love and the complete forgiveness he's made available for you. Others may mature very rapidly. It all depends on your level of surrender to the Holy Spirit and how much you understand that CHRIST COMPLETELY LIVES IN YOU. I've seen the Holy Spirit miraculously accelerate people's maturity when they are hungry, desperate and thirsty to learn about their new identity. This is because God feeds the hungry (John 6:35), he given water to the thirsty (Matthew 5:6) and he rewards those who diligently seek after him. Hebrews 11:6

Growth occurs when we absorb the truth about who we really are in our spirit and what we already possess in Christ.

LOVING OTHERS
FROM THE BOOK OF FIRST JOHN

The book of I John has a lot to say about the love of God and reflecting his love to others.

God is light and in him there is no darkness. If we claim to have fellowship with him but walk in darkness, then we lie and do not live by the truth. But if we walk in the light of his truth, we have fellowship with one another knowing that the blood of Jesus purifies us from all sin. I John 1:5-7

Because we love God, we love to obey his commands. The person who says, "I know him," but does not do what God commands is confused and the truth has not completely renewed their minds. But if anyone obeys God's word, God's love is truly made complete in them. This is how Christ lives through us. Whoever claims to be a Christian should strive to emulate the characteristics of Christ. I John 2:3-6

Anyone who claims to be in the light, but lives in strife with others, is still in darkness. Whoever loves others lives in the light and no darkness will ever make them stumble. I John 2:9-10

If anyone has material possessions and sees someone in need, but has no pity on them, how can the love of God be in them? I John 3:17

This is a commandment of God: to believe in the name of his Son, Jesus Christ, and to love one another as he has commanded us. This is how we know God spirit lives in us. I John 3:23 & 24

Dear friends, let us always, fervently and unconditionally love one another, this is the type of love that comes from God's spirit inside of us. Everyone who has been born of God has been filled with his love. Whoever has a difficult time loving others hasn't had a radiant revelation of God's nature. This is how God has expressed his love towards us: God loves us so much that he sent his Son as an atoning sacrifice for our sins. Release God's love out of your spirit and it will have a tremendous effect on you and others around you. I John 4:7-11

We love because he first loved us. If anyone proclaims that they love God but still has strife in their heart, then they have not had a clear revelation of the depth of God's true nature. I John 4:19 & 20

GO AND LOVE MY PEOPLE

Beloved, we're not going to be able to love others without releasing the love of God that's in our spirit. It has to come FROM God, TO US and then THROUGH US and finally OUT TO OTHERS. If you're running on empty, then stop and ask God for a refilling. You can only drive a car for so long without stopping and putting gas in it. Ask God for a refilling of his never ending supply of love, then go and love people the way God loves you.

Don't get tired of blessing and helping people. In time you will receive a great reward for your faith-filled words and actions. So take advantage of every opportunity in reflecting Christ's love towards others. Galatians 6:9 & 10

When you squeeze an orange, orange juice comes out. When you squeeze and apple, apple juice comes out. When trials and disappointments squeeze a person filled with God's Holy Spirit, then God's love comes out. Patience comes out during frustrating times and peace comes out as the storm rages around you. **You are God's representative, ambassador and a minister of reconciliation.** God wants the world to see and experience his godly character attributes through you. The world won't be able to understand us, but they will be drawn to us and to God. **Loving other people glorifies God. We are the extension of God's heart here on earth.** Don't just love the ones that you *choose* to love or that *deserve* your love. GO AND LOVE THEM ALL like God commands us to do. The Spirit of God will teach you how.

Make my joy complete by being like minded, having the same love for each other that I have for you, be united in spirit and purpose. Do nothing out of selfish ambitions or motives, be more concerned about others than yourself. Don't be so consumed about your own life, but get involved in the lives of others. Your attitude should be the same as Christ's attitude. Philippians 2:2-5

Remember you are a light in this dark world. You are like a bright city that can be seen in the distance on a dark night. Does a person put a bowl over a candle they've just lit (Matthew 5:14)? You have a constant flowing fountain of God's love to draw from. Go and shine the light of Christ to everyone around you. Loving people is going to take some time out of your schedule. It's going to challenge you. But if you will listen to the Holy Spirit he will give you many creative ways to love others.

If you truly desire to be successful at loving people God's way…then you will be. So as often as you can, go and tell people that you love them and that God loves them. Then do everything in your power to show them that he really does.

WHERE HAS ALL THE LOVE GONE?

Where has all the love gone? I don't see it anywhere around. The world is filled with relationships with no love, no commitment, no communication and no forgiveness. Each person has gone their own way, with their own goals and desires. Each person has a, "What can I get out of this relationship," mentality. Relationships cannot survive like this and most of them don't.

Where has all the love gone? Communication between people has become shallow and superficial. There is no time to connect or bond with each other anymore. Our neighbors we live by are complete strangers to us. They are people we just give a quick hello to going from our car to our house.

Where has all the love gone? People hide behind many masks. There's no time to just get real with each other. The truth is we don't have it all together. People have unresolved issues that keep their relationships distant, shallow and weak.

Where has all the love gone? The world has twisted our love and deflated our passion. The world's love is self-centered and conditional. When did people forget how to love? If you reach out and get your hand slapped repeatedly, then eventually I guess you just stop reaching out. The world's love is cold and calloused. There are so many hard hearts out there. The light is fading fast. Will anyone be the first to open up their heart, reach out to someone and dare to love?

Where has all the love gone? The conclusion is, you can only trust yourself. People are unloving and unforgiving. They are completely focused on themselves and their own life. At their core they really don't even like themselves very much. They love money, houses, cars and possessions. They put their faith and hope in these things. They invest their time and energy into these things rather than love, compassion, sharing and concern.

Where has all the love gone? Many have turned their backs on the light, the truth and their source of hope. People don't seek after God. They don't trust him because they don't know him. They ask themselves, "Will God let me down just like so many others have?" People have turned away from God's outstretched arms for far too long.

Where has all the love gone? It's in Heaven where it's always been. The source of love is in the heart of God. His love erases doubt, crushes fear, heals our pain and removes our sin. God's love came down from Heaven and showed us THE LIGHT, THE TRUTH and THE WAY. Reach out today and grasp hold of a love that will never let you go and soon you'll say, I know where all the love has gone...IT'S RIGHT HERE LIVING IN ME.

WORLDLY LOVE

This world's love is shallow and cold. There's no fire in the world's love. You can't feel the warmth of it against you. It's a hypocritical love because it originates in worldly concepts and philosophies. This type of love has just enough patience to exist with people and no more than that. This type of love only gives when it's been given to. Just under the surface of the world's love is a raging fighting spirit filled with judgment, condemnation and wrath.

People camouflage themselves so well with this superficial worldly love. It has all kinds of conditions attached to it. This love can mask over a lot of hidden self-righteousness. It's a religious type of love that makes people feel good about themselves. It loves the least amount possible when tolerating people. It's out there in the world and it's in our churches as well. This type of love does not wrap itself in forgiveness. You have to earn its forgiveness. It's an ugly, lonely, pitiful way to love.

I've worked in the secular field for over thirty-five years and I've seen people who have allowed the world to vacuum out all their love, passion and hope. They have been hurt by the world and they've built walls around themselves so that no one will ever hurt them again. They won't share even the smallest things with others. The truth is, they can't give to others what they don't have in them. Their spirit is dead. They've never opened their mouth so the God could breathe his breath of life into them. They never opened their heart to him so he could make their spirit leap back to life. Their hearts are cold, empty and dark.

GOD'S LOVE

God reaches out to us everyday so that we can know and experience the fullness of his love. God's love strips away hate and disarms our enemies. Hate is crushed under God's love. The love of God causes us to forget any offenses and forgive completely. **Let God love you completely and radically with no limits. Receive his love into your heart and then you'll be able to love him back and finally truly love others.** This scripture has helped me tremendously when it comes to resting in God's love.

Come to me all you who are weary and heavily burdened and I will give you rest. Take my yoke upon you and learn from me, for I have a gentle and compassionate heart and you will find rest for your souls. My yoke is easy and my burden is light. Matthew 11:28-30

People who have been hurt by others don't trust like they first did when they were a child. They don't let anyone in behind the walls they've built. People have so many hang-ups when it comes to letting God love them. Remember when Jesus told the disciples:

Do not forbid the children to come to me, for such is the kingdom of Heaven. Luke 18:16

These children just wanted to get close to Jesus. They wanted to be next to him, sit in his lap and touch the face of God. At first the disciples rebuked the children and the children didn't understand what the disciples were talking about. They didn't know there were rules and regulations about seeking God. THAT'S RELIGION! **Don't hinder God's free flowing love, power and presence because of pain, traditions, confusion and stubbornness.** Jesus told his disciples, "NO! NO! NO!

Don't do that! Just let them come to me." God wants us to trust and love him without limits. He wants us to come seeking, searching and to be curious about his nature.

STORY - Do Not Forbid The Children

During the Sunday morning worship time at my church, I briefly opened my eyes during a song and I saw two little girls at the altar dancing and praising God. WOW! This was awesome! They had these big beautiful smiles on their faces and they were holding hands and dancing. It's sad to say, but I've rarely seen people this happy and free when worshiping God. I've been on stage a number of times looking out at the congregation, so I know what you see can be very discouraging. I thought to myself, "Oh God, if only we could all be that free when worshiping you." Those two little girls taught me a lot about communing with God at a deeper level. The church has become so self conscious, busy and distracted during worship, I thought it was definitely a lesson we all needed to learn.

To my great surprise, the pastor did not agree with me. He did not perceive in the spirit what I saw. He had the most disgusted look on his face. He whispered over to the deacon and then the deacon came down and stopped the girls from praising and worshiping God and ushered them back to their seats.

Oh church, some days we just blow it. We totally miss what God has planned for us. My wife says when we all get to Heaven, we're all going to be little five year old black children (referring to the pigmentation of the skin). Why…maybe because she's white (referring to her light beige skin tone). Maybe it really will be like that, just to teach us that skin color demonstrates the diversity of

God's creativity. It's not a reason to hate and destroy one another. Why does my wife think we're all going to be children? Because children trust and love without limits. Children who are free in their spirit dance and enjoy life with each other. They believe with all their heart and that's exactly how God wants us to live out our faith. I believe Jesus was trying to teach his disciples something in this situation in Luke 18:16. Will we open our hearts and learn...is a question we answer everyday through our actions.

God says to us in his word:

Come to me my child, I will catch you.
Believe in me and every word that comes out
of my mouth. Every word I speak is the truth.
In fact, it is impossible for me to lie.
Only truth will come out of my mouth and
every promise that I speak will come to pass.
When I say, "I LOVE YOU", I really do.
You can trust in my love.
I will not reject you like the world has.
I created you.
I love your simple, unwavering trust that you have.
Chase after me and I will catch you
and show you my true nature.

If people would just let that word, written by the spirit of God, absorb into their heart, then a deep healing process would begin in them. Let Jesus' words wrap themselves around you like a blanket. Take them into your thirsty soul. Then he'll give you perfect peace and complete rest. He will give you rest on every side and in all circumstances. Hurting, controlling, dysfunctional people need to let down their guard, turn off the control force field they have around themselves and let God inside. Won't you let God heal everything about you today?

Moses said to God…."WHO AM I?" Exodus 3:11

One of the very first things a Christian needs to discover is WHO THEY ARE IN CHRIST. The Bookmarkers *I AM / HE SHALL BE CALLED, BY GOD'S GRACE, GOD KNOWS MY NAME* and *MY LITTLE CHILD* will remind you of who you are everyday. Your identity is your foundation for your Christian life.

I AM

ABOUNDING IN GRACE II Corinthians 9:8
ABLE Philippians 4:1
AN AMBASSADOR FOR CHRIST II Corinthians 5:20
ANOINTED II Corinthians 1:21
MADE RIGHTEOUS Romans 5:19
THE APPLE OF GOD'S EYE Zechariah 2:8
ALIVE Ephesians 2:4
CLAY IN THE POTTERS HANDS Jeremiah18:6
ANXIOUS FOR NOTHING Philippians 4:6
BORN AGAIN I Ptr. 1:23
NOT ASHAMED II Timothy 1:12
ADOPTED Ephesians 1:5
BLAMELESS I Corinthians 1:8
CHERISHED Ephesians 5:29
BAPTIZED INTO CHRIST I Corinthians 2:15
FREE John 8:36
BLOOD BOUGHT I Corinthians 6:19-20
BLESSED Ephesians 1:3
A CHILD OF GOD John1:12
CLEANSED I John 1:7,9
A CITIZEN OF HEAVEN Philippians 3:20
HIS Isaiah 43:1
COMPLETE IN CHRIST Colossians 2:10
CHOSEN I Peter 2:9
A CONQUEROR Romans 8:37
CALLED I Peter 5:10
CRUCIFIED WITH HIM Galatians 2:20
FAVORED Job 10:2
DELIVERED Psalm 107:6
DEAD TO SIN Romans 6:11
FORGIVEN Ephesians 1:7
A LIGHT IN A DARK PLACE Acts 13:47

A FELLOW CITIZEN OF HEAVEN Ephesians 2:19
INSEPARABLE FROM HIS LOVE Romans 8:35
GIVEN THE HOLY SPIRIT II Corinthians 1:2
HUMBLE Philip. 2:24
GLORIFIED WITH HIM II Thessalonians 2:14
FULL OF THE FRUIT OF THE SPIRIT Gal. 5:22,23
GRANTED GRACE IN CHRIST JESUS Romans 5:17
GIVEN AN ABUNDANT LIFE I John 4:9
SAVED Ephesians 2:8
HEALED I Peter 2:24
HEAVEN BOUND I Peter 1:4
HIS HANDIWORK Ephesians 2:10
ACCEPTED Ephesians 1:6
HONORED II Timothy 2:21
LIBERATED Romans 6:23
HOLY Ephesians 1:4
COMFORTED Jeremiah 31:13
IN CHRIST I Corinthians 1:30
JUSTIFIED Acts 13:39
LOST, BUT NOW I'M FOUND Luke 19:10
A NEW CREATION II Corinthians 5:17
CONFIDENT I John 4:17
GUILTLESS AND NOT CONDEMNED Romans 8:1
PLEASING TO GOD Psalm 149:4
THE HEAD Deuteronomy 28:13
A MOUNTAIN MOVER Mark 11:22
LOVED John 3:16
MADE BY HIM Psalm 100:3
NEAR TO GOD Ephesians 2:13
NEVER FORSAKEN Hebrews 13:5
JOYFUL Philippians 4:4
NOT A SLAVE TO SIN Romans 8:1
A LIGHT John 8:12

AN OVERCOMER *I John 5:4,5*
PEACEFUL *Philippians 4:7*
PROTECTED *Psalm 91:14*
PROVIDED FOR *Matthew 6:33*
QUALIFIED *Colossians 1:12*
YIELDED TO GOD *Romans 6:13*
RAISED UP WITH CHRIST *Eph 2:6*
WALKING IN HIS LIGHT *I Jn. 1:7*
RECONCILED TO GOD *Rom. 5:10*
A ROYAL PRIESTHOOD *I Ptr. 2:9*
RENEWED *II Corinthians 4:16*
A SAINT OF GOD *Psalm 34:9*
SANCTIFIED *I Corinthians 6:11*
A TEMPLE *I Corinthians 3:16*
TRANSFORMED *II Corinthians 3:18*
REDEEMED *Galatians 3:13*
TREASURED *Psalm 83:3*
TRIUMPHANT *II Corinthians 2:14*

(FRONT OF BOOKMARKER)

HE SHALL BE CALLED

A GIFT FROM GOD John 3:16
A SACRIFICE Ephesians 5:2
THE BRIGHT AND MORNING STAR Revelation 22:16
IMAGE OF THE INVISIBLE GOD Col. 1:15
MASTER Mark 12:14
THE BEGINNING AND THE END Revelation 21:6
ARM OF THE LORD Isaiah 51:9
AN OFFERING Luke 4:34
A SURE FOUNDATION Isa. 28:16
GREAT HIGH PRIEST Heb. 4:14
MOST HOLY Daniel 9:24
ONLY BEGOTTEN SON John 3:16
LIGHT OF THE WORLD John 9:5
KING OF KINGS I Timothy 6:15
ADVOCATE I John 2:1
ALMIGHTY Revelation 19:15
AUTHOR AND FINISHER OF OUR FAITH Heb. 12:2
BREAD OF LIFE John 6:35
DELIVERER Romans 11:26
THE ROCK OF MY SALVATION II Samuel 22:47
CHIEF CORNERSTONE I Peter 2:6
I AM John 8:58
EMMANUEL - GOD WITH US Matthew 1:23
LORD OF THE SABBATH Lk. 6:5
RIGHTEOUS JUDGE II Tim. 4:8
THE SON OF THE HIGHEST Luke 1:32
SON OF GOD Luke 1:35
SERVANT Philippians 2:7
FAITHFUL & TRUE Revelation 19:11
MESSIAH Daniel 9:25
GOOD SHEPHERD John 10:11

OUR MEDIATOR Hebrews 12:24
HOPE OF GLORY Colossians 1:27
OUR SHIELD John 6:51
TEACHER John 3:2
OUR PEACE Ephesians 2:14
LIVING WATER John 4:10
LAMB OF GOD John 1:36
LORD OF ALL Acts 10:36
REDEEMER Isaiah 59:20
OUR INTERCESSOR Hebrews 7:25
PHYSICIAN Luke 4:23
OUR REFUGE FROM THE STORM Isaiah 5:4
SAVIOR OF THE WORLD I John 4:14
RESURRECTION AND THE LIFE John 1:25
OUR ROCK AND OUR FORTRESS Psalm 31:3
WONDERFUL COUNSELOR, MIGHTY GOD,
EVERLASTING FATHER, PRINCE OF PEACE Isa. 9:6
GOD MANIFEST IN THE FLESH I Timothy 3:16
THE WORD Revelation 19:13
MAN FROM HEAVEN I Corinthians 15:48
A QUICKENING SPIRIT I Corinthians 15:45
THE WAY, THE TRUTH AND THE LIFE John 14:6

JESUS CHRIST THE LORD

(Back Of Bookmarker)

I AM / HE SHALL BE CALLED was compiled by Eric Johnson

These words are a phenomenal reminder of who we are IN CHRIST and who Jesus is to the world. There are many bookmarkers in my collection that I feel need to be read everyday and this is certainly one of them. The more we read and believe the more we will be transformed into the likeness of Christ. This bookmarker is an awesome collection of scriptural truths about us and our savior. Remember, your actions will always follow your beliefs. When you begin to believe what God says about you to be true, then you'll begin to act on those beliefs.

How a person thinks about themselves...
is what they'll soon become. Proverbs 23:7

I want you to start a new habit. First thing in the morning, I want you to stand in front of the mirror and read the *I AM* bookmarker I've compiled. I want you to look in the mirror and read that information about yourself. Let it absorb deep into your spirit. **If God can convince you, through his word, of everything you already divinely possess, then you'll start acting on those new beliefs about your true identity and the power and gifts of God will be ushered in through your renewed faith.**

That's one of the reasons God has you reading this book right now, so that you will believe what God says about you to be true. God only speaks the truth, he cannot lie. If God says you're TREASURED, CHERISHED and LOVED by him, THEN YOU REALLY ARE! That's why I wrote this book, so that you would trust God completely with your life, believe in the truth of his word and know that he will be there for you everyday through his Holy Spirit. This book boldly proclaims what the Lord Jesus Christ has done for the entire world. If you'll go a little further in your faith, God will meet you there in _your_ hunger, _your_ desire, _your_ desperation, in _your_ expectation, in _your_ hope and in _your_ faith-filled positive words.

You'll start SPEAKING things you never spoke before.
You'll start DOING things you never did before.
You'll start THINKING things you never imagined before.

You'll start LOVING people
who you never thought you could love.
Instead of holding on to offenses, you'll start
FORGIVING people instantly and completely.

The truth about you and God being together forever, will set you free to live a God glorifying, victorious, powerful, thriving life. John 8:32

WE ARE HIS TO BE LOVED

God loves us unconditionally, therefore there is nothing that you can do that would make him love you more and there is nothing that you can do that would make him love you less. God is love. It's his nature to love without caution or restraint or conditions. We will always be loved by him.

His love is unchanging. He won't love us any better when we become better. He loves us one hundred percent right now as we are. The dimensions of God's love for us is higher than the Heavens are above the earth. His love does not change even if we have no plans to change. What needs to change is our ability to receive his love. **So the choice is yours, will you open your heart to him right now and receive more of his love than you've ever experienced before?** Give him your whole heart today child of God. Give him your obstacles and pain that stand in the way. He'll remove them and give you rest that you've never experienced before. God loves us one hundred percent as we are right at this moment. So let yourself be loved by him.

Allow God's love to saturate your heart. This is why he created us. This is why he has set his gaze towards us. He adores you. He's crazy about you. He wants us to live like people who are loved outrageously. God wants us to understand, receive and express this radical, out of this world type of love. God's love is so awesome that all the poets throughout history could barely describe it. God will love us all the days of our life because that is who he is. He doesn't know how to be any different towards you.

God's love comes to set us free from ourselves and to set us free from how we see ourselves. His love comes to set us free from rejection, shame, low self-esteem, despair and from self-abuse. When God looks at us, he sees someone who he loves outrageously. God has so much to say to us and so many places to take us in his heart. But we can't go there unless we allow him to love us completely. His love for us will break every barrier and crush every wall that we've built around ourselves. **God's love is the most power force that has ever touched the human heart.** So allow yourself to be loved.

I hope your level of understanding will one day reach God's level of love for you. When you finally believe in God's unconditional love and receive it into your heart, it will change you in every facet of your expression towards him and others. The words written on the *BY GOD'S GRACE* bookmarker will help you get a better understanding of how much God loves you.

BY GOD'S GRACE

*I am dearly loved and have been chosen by God.
He has called me to be compassionate, forgiving and to
reflect the love of Christ to this hurting world.
Colossians 3:12; Ephesians 4:32*

*By God's grace every sin of mine has been forgiven.
I am free from the condemning voice of the enemy.
I am God's holy creation and I stand blameless
in his sight. Romans 5:1, 6:1-6*

*God adopted me as his child because he loves me.
He has placed his seal upon me. I am a fellow citizen of
Heaven and a member of God's household.
Ephesians 1:4 & 13, 2:19*

*God has enlightened my heart, given me wisdom and
understanding that I might know him completely.
Ephesians 1:8 & 17*

*I have been made alive through Jesus Christ. I have
God's mighty power and strength working in my inner
being. Ephesians 1:18, 2:5 & 6*

*I have direct access to God through his Holy Spirit.
I can approach him with freedom and confidence.
Ephesians 2:18, 3:12*

*I have been given salvation, love, peace and divine truth.
They are like an impenetrable suit of armor I wear
to protect me from this dark world. Ephesians 6:14*

*I have been redeemed and forgiven of all my sins.
The debt against me was canceled, removed, blotted out
and forgotten forever. Colossians 1:14*

*I have the right to come boldly before the throne of God
to find mercy and grace in my time of need. Heb. 4:16*

I have been given the mind of Christ. My mind is full of patience, kindness, gentleness and self control. I will show the world the love of Christ through my peaceful attitude and gentle actions. Galatians 5:22

I have the life of God inside of me and I will walk in that new revelation everyday. Romans 6:4

God has done a great work in me, so that I can accomplish his good and perfect will, which is my destiny. Philippians 2:13

I have been given the grace to live a life that is pleasing to the Lord, bearing fruit in every good work, growing in the knowledge of God and being strengthened with all power according to his glorious might. Colossians 1:10 & 11

I have been rescued from the pit of despair and brought into the kingdom of light. Colossians 1:13

I have been appointed by God to serve. He has ordered my steps and supernaturally positioned me to accomplish mighty things. I Timothy 1:12

compiled by Eric Johnson

Your comprehension of God's love is directly proportional to your hunger for his love. Dear saints of God, if we would just hunger and then comprehend how much God loves us, it would transform the core of our spirit and radically impact the world we live in. It would change the intensity and focus of our passion. It will change the way you think, your attitude, self-image and the words that come out of your mouth. It will affect how much you smile, what you read, what you look at and how you interpret life. God's love completely and totally transforms people. There is no area of your character that God's love will not altar.

If God had a mountain of diamonds, rubies, emeralds, gold and silver; he would cast them all away if you walked up to him. You are his creation, he treasures you. He calls you his friend. He adores you and cherishes you. You were created for his pleasure and glory. **You were purchased by sinless, holy, perfect, divine blood...God's blood.** A very high price was paid so that you could be reconciled to him. He adopted you into his family so that you now have legal citizenship in Heaven.

*Nothing can ever separate you
from the love of God! Romans 8:39*

*I will protect them and bless them and fill them with my love, they will be great because of me, says the Lord.
I will love them forever and be kind to them always.
Psalm 89:24 & 28*

*God's love is so great toward us that he treats us
like we are his very own children. I John 3:1
Even while people were enjoying their sinful nature,
God demonstrated his great love towards us by
sending Christ to die for us. Romans 5:8*

God showed us how much he loved us by sending his only Son into the world, so that we might have experience eternal life through him. This is real, pure, perfect, unmerited love. The way the world loves is not even comparable to the way God loves us, because he sent his Son as a sacrifice to take care of the sin issue between God and mankind and reconciled us to himself. I John 4:9-10

For God so loved the world that he gave his only Son to die for us, so that everyone who believes in him will not perish but have eternal life to enjoy everyday. God did not send his son into the world to condemn people, but so that people could be saved by Christ's message, actions and sacrifice. John 3:16 & 17

Do you see the connection between God's love and the sacrifice of Jesus for our sins? God wants us to do four things with his love.

- God wants us to READ about his love in the bible...then meditating on it and opening our heart to the Holy Spirit's leading. When you allow God's word into your mind you allow God's love in your heart.
- God wants us to UNDERSTAND his love...by hungering for more of him and asking for wisdom.
- God wants us to RECEIVE his love...by letting go of hurt, pain, confusion, religion and control.
- God wants us to REFLECT his love to others...by showing genuine compassion and appreciation towards them.

STORY – A Day At the Beach With God

One time we went on a weekend trip to Lake Michigan. I asked God for good weather on this one particular day that we were going to go to the beach. But unfortunately the forecast called for thunderstorms and the dark clouds were already rolling in. We contemplated going home early that day because the weather looked so lousy and the weather report was so dismal. Then my daughter said, "But what about our day at the beach?" I realized at that moment how important to her that day at the lake was. So we decided to continue, as planned to Lake Michigan. I started to pray to God.

Lord this is just between you and me. It's just one of those things I need to see right now. Is it critical? NO. Is it a necessity? NO. It's just something my family would love. I just need to know Lord that you would change a weather front coming in for your children that you love.

The weather looked so bad that many people were leaving the beach as we were walking down to it. When we got down to the beach, a mysterious opening began to develop in the dark sky and it headed towards us. Clear blue sky stayed over us the entire day. I had prayed for God to bless us with great weather and he did. Guess what, the water was unusually warm that day also. PRAISE THE LORD! All day my wife and I kept commenting on how beautiful the weather was and how great God is.

I thought to myself, "God did you do this for me? God do you love me that much that you changed the air pressure, temperature and all the necessary climate conditions for us to have a great day at the beach?" I felt God in my spirit say, "You wouldn't ask that question if you understood the depth of my love for you."

Just as an earthly father would give good gifts to his children, how much more does your heavenly Father love and care for you. Matthew 11:17

I love that part where God says, *"how much more."* That's the part God wants us to completely comprehend. He wants us to know *how much more* he loves us than anything else in all his creation. He wants us to realize *how much more* he has done and will do than any earthly father ever could.

Many times it seems like it's hard to fully understand and receive God's love. Receiving God's love may be just as simple as to STOP REJECTING IT. For some people it's hard for them to feel love. Maybe it has something to do with the way they were raised. Maybe the words I LOVE YOU weren't really said in the home where you grew up. I challenge you to stop rejecting God and receive his love in a completely new and extraordinary way.

GOD KNOWS MY NAME

You know my heart and you know everything about me.
You know when I sit down and when I stand up.
You know all my thoughts throughout the day.
You know the path ahead of me and show me
where to kneel and rest in your presence.
You watch over me wherever I go.
You know every word that comes out of my mouth.
You go ahead of me to guide the way
and chase after me when I wonder off.
Your hand of blessing is always on my head.
Your knowledge is too wonderful for me to understand.
I never want to escape from your presence.
If I go up to Heaven, you are there.
If I go down to the depths of the sea, you are there.
In the morning you're there to greet me.
If I go to a far away country your strong hand guides me.
If I find myself in darkness, you are a light to my path.
In my mother's womb you formed all my inner most parts.
I will praise you because I am
fearfully and wonderfully made.
Your workmanship is marvelous, how well I know it.
You knew me before I was born, every moment of my life
was laid out before you. How precious are your thoughts
about me, I can't even count them, they out number
the grains of sand on the seashore.
You are my God and you're always near.
Search me Lord, know my heart and reveal
to me your new spirit that lives within me.

(Adapted from Psalm 139:1-23 and complied by Eric Johnson)

ARE YOU ASHAMED OF JESUS CHRIST?

Some people feel that God is a very personal and private subject and they should just speak to God when they are alone with him. They rarely mention the name of Jesus to anyone, not even to their family members or others who are close to them. They let other people believe what they want to believe so they don't offend anyone. They believe everyone needs to find God in their own way, by themselves. The subject of God or Jesus rarely comes out of their mouth because their faith is a very private subject. This type of thinking does not align with the truth from God's word.

The good news of the gospel message is not a private subject! Mankind being reconciled to God is GOOD NEWS and we're supposed to share that GOOD NEWS with everyone. God in you is supposed to be attracting others to God through you.

Jesus said, *"Come follow me and I will make you fishers of men" (Matthew 4:19).* You'll never catch anything if you don't throw your line out. Your actions will always follow your beliefs. If you don't ever confess Jesus as Lord publicly, then what does that say about your faith in him? Here are the words of Jesus:

If you confess me to people, then I will confess you before my Father in Heaven. If you do not confess me before others, then I will not confess you before my Father in Heaven. Matthew 10:32

This is the Apostle Paul speaking:

I am not ashamed of the gospel of Christ, because it reveals the truth about the life transforming power of God's salvation for anyone who will believe.
Romans 1:16

Holy Spirit filled, born-again, fire-baptized children of God are not ashamed or embarrassed about telling people what the Lord Jesus has done for them. The Holy Spirit doesn't want you to be quiet, backward and timid. He wants you to continually speak the glories of God out of your mouth. **The Holy Spirits mission is to establish God's kingdom *in us*, so that others may see, understand and experience God also. If you're not an active participant in this process, then you're missing out on a huge part of your divine purpose.**

You are my children, I created you to bring me glory.
Isaiah 43:7

Everything you think, say and do should glorify God.
Romans 6:13

The Holy Spirit does not teach us to be a loud mouth or arrogant and preach down to people. He doesn't teach us to judge, criticize or condemn. That's not his way. That's not the Holy Ghost boldness I'm talking about. The Holy Spirit speaks the truth to people after it's been saturated with the love of God. Love is his favorite subject. He doesn't bother getting into arguments with people because he always speaks the truth about God. He speaks the truth about you and he speaks the truth about every other subject in life. **He's not afraid to confront people and you shouldn't be afraid either, because he lives in you. Let the Holy Spirit pull open that jaw you've wired shut and he will amaze you with what comes out of you.**

COMMUNICATION AND RELATIONSHIPS

My wife and I will be talking and I will be responding back to her. It seems like we're having a good conversation, at least from my perspective (a man's perspective). Then she will say to me, "You're not listening to me." I'm thinking in my head, "What is she talking about?" I am right here having a conversation with her. A few sentences later she will say it again, "You're not listening to me." I don't understand, I'm sitting right next to her, speaking to her and trying to solve all her problems. But again she will say, "You're not listening to me again."

My point is this, people have trouble communicating even when their standing right next to each other face to face. How are we going to communicate effectively with a supernatural being like God, whom we can't see, hear or touch? I've heard a lot of people say, "I don't feel like God hears me when I pray." Maybe you need to change your approach. Have you ever tried being still and listening to God? Maybe he's trying to speak to you, but you're not listening. Maybe he's already heard you and now he's trying to respond to you. **Sometimes our prayer life is like a tornado. It touches the ground for only a minute and then it's gone.** People spend a lot of time telling God about all their worries and fears, then they beg him for everything on their list...AND THEN IT'S OVER! That's all the time they have for him until their next crisis comes along. Soon after that, their so-called prayer time becomes even less and less. They become disillusioned with a God that never seems to hear or answer their requests. Christian soldier, we need to slow down. We need to be still and know that the Lord is God. Great relationships have great two way communication.

Great communication is not only comprised of good speaking skills but also great listening skills. God is already an excellent communicator, so it's you and I that need to listen with our heart, soul and spirit.

My sheep hear my voice, they feel the security of my presence and they follow me. John 10:27
Call to me and I will answer you and show you great and mighty things. Jeremiah 33:3

How much time do you spend just simply waiting and listening for God to speak to you in your spirit? What kind of relationship are you going to have with him, if you're the one doing all the talking all the time? Can you imagine how exhausting it must be for God; with everyone telling him what they want, how they want things to happen and what their opinion is on every subject. Many people yell at him because their mad and frustrated. Doesn't that sound similar to how Jesus was treated? **All God ever wanted to do was save us, heal us, bless us and show us how to be close to him forever.**

Do you know how big God's complaint department must be? Is your relationship with God like a genie in a lamp, who's there to grant your request, but never seems to ever respond to you? Maybe that's why people feel so distant from God. He's trying to teach them about his character and how to connect with him. Many people just never seem to be able to find the time to experience the most important relationship they will ever encounter.

We are the one's who hinder God from flooding into our lives, because we don't surrender ALL the areas of our life to him.

<u>God says to us in his word:</u>
I will stick closer than a brother. Proverbs 18:24
I will never leave you or forsake you. Hebrews 13:5
We were all distant from God, but now we have been
brought close to him, because of the atonement
of the Lord Jesus Christ. Ephesians 2:13

I don't know how close you want to be to God, but I do know God wants to be close to you. He has repeated himself many times regarding this intimacy in the bible. God said a number of times in the Old Testament that he is a jealous God. This shows us that God has feelings also. God can be angered, outraged and lonely. He is also loving, patient and compassionate. When we turn our backs on God...he hurts inside... because his creation has rejected him.

STORY – Never Alone

A lot of times I'll find myself falling into a very busy life style. When I finally realize that I've been neglecting that important time with God, I'll find a quiet place where I can focus on him. I feel bad sometimes to even come before him and ask for his presence to surround me, because I've been so busy with all the stuff that life has thrown at me. I know that God is always with me... but sometimes I'm not always with him.

One time I said, "Lord...what right do I have to come to you and expect you to just come flooding in and show up at my front door? Just because I am now ready to speak to you. What right do I have to come before you just because I've finally found few minutes out of the day to connect with you. That doesn't really seem fair to you. You have always been so very patient with me. If you're there Lord..."

Right then God stopped me in the middle of my prayer and said to me, "If I'm there, you ask. I have always been here inside of you. I'm always patiently waiting for you and me to celebrate life together. Don't you know that I go before you, to lead you into your day? I walk behind you, to catch you when you fall. I'm above you, watching over you like a shepherd watches over their sheep. I walk beside you to comfort you and encourage you like a friend. I am beneath you to lift you up throughout your day. I told you that I would never leave you or forsake you. When I said I will stick closer than a brother...I MEANT IT. Believe this...I am here and I am listening, but I have something important to say to you first:

I LOVE YOU! I LOVE YOU! I LOVE YOU!
I LOVE YOU! I LOVE YOU! I LOVE YOU!
I LOVE YOU! I LOVE YOU! I LOVE YOU!"

Do you understand why I believe the way I do? This book is filled with my personal experiences with God and all the many ways he has revealed himself to me. I wrote this book to let you know that God is just as passionate about you. He's ready to reveal himself to you in many new and extraordinary ways.

I LOVE HIM BECAUSE HE FIRST LOVED ME

Love the Lord with all of your heart, with all your soul, with all your mind and with all your strength.
Mark 12:30

God wants us to love him wholeheartedly, without any reservations, because that's how he loves us. The love that we give to God originated from him.

I used to love God in the same way I love chocolate cake. But now all these many years later, I love him so much more. The love I have for God now comes in a different container. It shines a little brighter than I ever thought it would. You see before I was willing to learn about God, but I wasn't willing to change that much. After a few years of learning about how much he really loves me, I was willing to change, but my growth was very slow. After a few more years of serving God, reading his word and having greater revelations of him through supernatural experiences, I finally reached the point in my life where I was willing to grow at any cost. Have you ever felt this way about God? **I'm sure you love God in your own way, but we need to love God his way.**

With ALL of our heart. (Passion and will)
With ALL of our soul. (Personality and attitude)
With ALL of our mind. (Thoughts and consciousness)
With ALL of our strength. (Time, money,
energy and actions)

Matthew 22:37, Mark 12:30 & Luke 10:27

True love means sacrificing something for someone else. **When I began to meditate on the tremendous sacrifice that Jesus made for me, it changed how I responded to God.** When I realized that everything he suffered through was because he loved me, then I began to love differently. It's a love that is out of this world, because it's not from this world. Jesus taught this lesson to his disciples.

Two men owed money to a certain moneylender. One owed him five hundred silver coins and the other fifty. Neither of them had the money to pay him back, so the moneylender cancelled the debts that both men owed. Now which man will love the lender more? Simon replied, "I suppose the one who had the bigger debt cancelled." Jesus said, "You are right." Then he turned toward the woman and said to Simon, "Do you see this woman? When I came into your house, you did not give me any water for my feet, but she has wet my feet with her tears and wiped them with her hair. You did not give me a kiss, but this woman, from the time I entered, has not stopped kissing my feet. You did not put oil on my head, but she has poured perfume all over my feet.
I tell you, her many sins have been forgiven for she loved much." Luke 7:41-47

This woman's entire body became a worship vessel. She knew what she had been forgiven of and she loved God with all she had within her. When you begin to understand what you have been forgiven of and the price that was paid for you, then you'll begin to love with intensity and passion. Can you imagine how sad God must feel when we don't love him back?

If you're too busy for God then you're just too busy. Take some time to discover God's love and it will stretch the limits of your eart and emotions. God promises us that if we will put forth any effort at all, he will reveal himself to us in a way we can understand.

Jesus said, "If anyone loves me, they will obey my teachings, because my Father has come down from Heaven and make his home in their heart." John 14:23

Conclusion

When we try to love people without the help of the Holy Spirit it becomes a conditional, fragile, limited, imperfect love. When we love people with the love that comes from God, it's a perfect love. It's a love that perseveres and hopes for the best in others. It's not a jealous love, it's not easily angered.

The distance between God's love and the world's love is an entire universe apart. But if you'll surrender your heart to him, his love will travel from the edge of the universe to you in just a fraction of a second and fill your heart completely.

The heart of God is the only place you can truly find rest for your soul. The world's love is driven by the flesh, but God's love came down from Heaven and walked among us through the Lord Jesus Christ. Don't miss out on the most awesome love you'll ever experience. Chase after it, embrace it and never let go of God's perfect, unconditional, out of this world, mind blowing, heart healing love.

This book has touched on some foundational principles for you to live a life of faith that's exciting, passionate and filled with God's love and divine power.
If you would like to read more, here is a complete list of all my books found at amazon.com:

Me & God - Together At Last
Is God Angry With The Church
Enjoying The Fruit That's In Your Spirit
God Loves You
Prayer That Touched God's Heart

My email address:
nvmjohnson@yahoo.com

Facebook:
https://www.facebook.com/eric.johnson.58555

Twitter:
https://twitter.com/nvtjohnson1

Please check out my life changing blogs with over 10,000 views:
www.blogger.com/profile/02794291088369664066

www.ingramcontent.com/pod-product-compliance
Lightning Source LLC
Chambersburg PA
CBHW060955040426
42445CB00011B/1166